Sometimes I Weep

Ken Walsh

SOMETIMES I WEEP

Prayers and Meditations

SCM PRESS LTD

334 01576 6

First published 1973
by SCM Press Ltd
56 Bloomsbury Street London

© SCM Press Ltd 1973

Printed in Great Britain by
Cox & Wyman Ltd, London, Reading and Fakenham

Contents

To me God is the spirit who created and who controls the universe. I say 'who' because my experience of God has been as with a person with whom I can communicate. God is love, and he is in all things. His laws are built into our bodies and minds; the laws of nature are his laws.

I know most of God as love through the life and death of Jesus Christ. I know most of God as truth, beauty and order through nature. God is reality, and in him I have complete and utter confidence.

1   *About myself and God*

Thanks

I'm coming good again, Lord,
Thanks;
I can breathe the air,
Soak in the smiles –
It's good to be alive.

I share it with you

Lord,
I've made a mistake
And now everyone's tired and crabby,
And the poor kids catch it.

I reasoned things out,
Then acted on impulse
And was glad – at first.
Now, maybe facing the emptiness
And disappointment in the beginning
Might have been better than this.

I tried to force it
And it didn't work.

So now
I share it
With you –
All of it.

To enjoy the rain

Lord,
Why do we only see you
As an escape,
As a place to hide?

Why do we see your world
As all bad,
All threatening?

And think that all
Truth and goodness
Live in us,
And depend entirely on us?

Why are we so arrogant?

Lord, help us not to
Look on you as an umbrella,
But as someone who
Helps us to enjoy
The rain.

By our actions

Lord,
We have ignored your laws –
Your laws of nature.
And now
We pray, asking you
To take away the consequence
Of our neglect.

Take away our blindness –
And help us to bear the responsibility
Of our neglect,
By our actions.

Keeping in touch

Surely I could keep in touch
With you, Lord,
Better than I do?

Now I'm calm and at peace,
But come tomorrow
Off I'll go tearing into things:
Arguing, pushing, listening,
And then I'll come home
Worn out.

Why can't I be aware of you
Like now –
Only all day through?
So that I'm calm and receptive
Most of the time anyway.

And if I'm in touch with you
Then those with whom I come in contact
Will know you're there too.

I suppose that's one of the greatest things
I could do –
To act as a live channel
For you.

The good points first

O God,
May I look at a painting
(or any creative work)
And see its good points
First –
See the artist's struggle to create,
And then note, but see past
The mistakes.

May I learn to see people
In the same way.

May I look at people
As I see myself.

Above our problems

Oh God,
Here I am again – miserable.
Miserable to the depths,
Looking at everything selfishly,
Just from my own view point –
It's not much of a view.
Feeling hemmed in by problems
And weariness,
Unable to escape
To the sunshine.

But I am being narrow and self-centred,
If I look around
I'm far better off than most –
I have more love,
More opportunities,
More shafts of sunlight.

Forgive my sniffling and whining,
Help me back on to my feet,
So that I in turn may extend my hand
And help others rise
Above their problems.

At our own speed

We break our necks
Trying to be 'with it',
Or trying to be what we think
Is 'with it'.

And then we feel ill at ease, in
Garments
We're not ready to wear.

O Lord, may we seek you
Being our own ordinary selves –
Growing at our own speed
Whatever it is.

Which storm to choose

O God,
I come seeking a simple answer
To a complex problem –
And there is none.
There is only a choice of difficult answers.

Lord,
Show me which one to choose,
And be with me in the storm.

Where I'll find you

O God,
Where are you?

Here.
Where?

Here, in this person
And this person and this person.

But Lord,
I loathe some of these people.

I know,
But this is where
You'll find me.

I remember now

O Lord, I look at the mountain
And I tremble,
In fear of the long, hard climb
And the many obstacles.

I fear I'll slip and fall
And hurt myself
And maybe others;
Or that I'll get lost,
Or be unequal to the tasks.

I forget you –
And how you climbed.

I know,
I'm sorry,
I remember now.

As you meant them

O God,
That sex could find its right place
Like the buds on the chestnut tree,
That men could be fit like the blackbird
Poised in the cold, sharp wind,
That things could be
As you meant them,
Beautiful, healthy and free.

Tremendous!

Lord,
Are you receiving me?
I'm having a whale of a time,
It's tremendous!

Show me what prayer is

Lord,
I couldn't pray like that,
I'm not involved enough in the issue,
But then neither is he.

There I go
Being like that pharisee again,
Aren't I, Lord?

You said, 'Judge not, that ye be not judged',
And
'By their fruits shall ye know them.'

Show me what prayer is, Lord,
What forms it can take,
And the extent and the limit
Of what
I can pray about.

Is it what you want?

Lord,
This church service is beautiful,
Cultured and refined –
But is it what you want?

For this culture is not available
To a large number of people in this city.

Should we have worship
At different cultural levels?

Lord,
Didn't you come to heal our divisions?

Take away this fear

Lord,
If I have to die
Let me die;
But please,
Take away this fear.

In which direction

O God,
You know my situation –
How things are at work
How things are with my family
How things are with my health;
Show me where to go – on – from here, Lord,
Show me the way.

I don't ask to see the end of the road
Or even all the road,

Just enough, so that I'll know
In which direction
To move, now.

Where goodness ends and evil begins

Lord,
Do you mind if I'm honest with you?
Foolish question, I know
But so often I seem to see things differently
From those around me,
That I don't speak my thoughts –
I fear to differ, to offend,

And now I find I'm approaching you
In the same way.

You see it's all connected with this huge institutional church,
And the individuals outside it.

The very fact that we can afford well-cut suits,
That the girls up front attend our expensive church school,
That our choir sings only respectable church music,
Means we are creating and have created, divisions
In your world.
We've shut people out
By our riches –
And all this and more
In your name.

Lord, guide me,
Show me where goodness ends
And evil begins.

So that I might find you

O God,
Help me not to take myself
Too seriously,
Help me to let go –
To let go of my ambitions
         my selfish loves
         my fears,
So that I might find you –

In the people I meet.

What we mean

Thanks for the world, Lord,
It's beaut,
It really is;
This pop music is groovy –
It makes me feel alive.

These people are talking and singing
About me, my world,
You, your world,
Our world, Lord.

Some say, you only tune in
To church music;
I can't believe it.
This is your world
And I think you love it
As much as I do.

When will we learn
That what we mean
Is much more important
Than the words and the sounds we use
To convey that meaning?

I depend on you

O God,
In all this confusion
You're the only one
That's real.

You're my firm foundation.

On you I can depend,
In you I find,
Peace
Strength
Truth
And beauty.

In you
I can go on
No matter what the future holds,
For you have
Past
Present
Future
In your hands.

I can unload my pain, now,
And depend on you.
I can trust myself
And the future.
Thank you.

I'm not afraid of the future, now, God,
In fact I might even enjoy it.

So must I

It's funny, Lord, isn't it?
I mean
We feel guilty about things we needn't
And we don't feel guilty
About things we should,
And few of us would agree
On which was which anyway.

You must get tired of hearing me say,
I'm sorry.
I suppose you'd rather I did something
About the things I say I'm sorry for,
Or that I shut up
And learned to live with myself?

You accept me –
So must I.

I need you now

O God,
Guide me,
For I am a blind man
And I cannot see,
I am a deaf man
And I cannot hear,
I am a fearful man
And I cannot find the way.

Come close, Lord,
So that I can find you.

I am lost in a jungle:
Of pressures and noises,
Buildings and people,
Committees and decisions,
Praises and guilts.

I need you, God,
Now.

To pay the price

Lord,
Why should I have to upset the boss at work
Having to raise the unpleasant side of an issue
That's being avoided?
Why do I have to do the criticizing?
After all I'm a married man
With four children;
I mean if I lose this job
What about the children, the house payments?

Lately in books and films I've come across
The man who tried to be honest
So upset the others
That they either killed him
Or he had to leave.
But where to?
And then the same thing all over again?
More upset people.
I mean if I were single
I could continue to move –
But someday I'd have to stop.

I don't want to die, Jesus,
I don't want to be a hero
Or a martyr –
Nor do I want to hide.
If you say fight
I'll fight,
But sometimes I get tired fighting –

I've been letting off steam, Jesus,
Sometimes the pressure is too much.

Now I've unloaded it again.
All right, I'll stand
And do what I have to.
Help me to pay the price.
I accept the peace and freedom
You offer.

Amen.

A key

O God,
It is just like you have given me
A key
To a room full of answers.

I'll go

O God,
When I consider
What you are asking
I shudder,
I feel panic.

Me to question
These ancient and tried beliefs?
These respected institutions?
Me to question
And probably upset,
These powerful and formidable
People?

I must remind myself
You only ask what I am capable of,
And that you are with me –
I'll go,
Thank you
Father.

The only road

Oh Lord,
These days are no different
From any others,
My problems are no different
From anyone else's,
The problems of these times
Are the same
As the problems of other times.

The conditions may be different,
The struggles are the same –
Power versus conscience,
Lust versus love.
There is no fighting without wounds,
Scars, blood,
There is no victory without fighting,
To be in the struggle is the only road –
All else is emptiness.

It is the struggle you lived
(And died) through,
And like your disciples
I'm often afraid
And run away.

I seek peace

Lord,
I seek peace
And there's only fighting,
I seek friends
And I find enemies,
I seek rest
And the work is endless,
I seek escape –
And there is none.

Lord,
I seek you –
And I find you.
Thank you.

Answered

O God, you have always answered –
I have asked,
You have answered.

Just like breathing

Lord,
How seriously I have taken myself,
Fretting over this and that,
How am I going to manage it?
What will people think ...?

When will I learn
To relax, to let go,
To trust you,
Just like so many
So-called uneducated people do?

Naturally,
Just like breathing,
Simply,
Almost like taking you for granted –
Knowing you're always there.

The rock

I'm all right now
Thank you, Father,
I can feel the rock
Under my feet again.

2   *About the church*

Christianity

Peace in my trouble,
And trouble in my peace.
God in me
And I in God,
God in everything
And everything in God,
God loving me exactly as I am, now,
And all other men like this too,
(Even the ones I don't like
And who don't believe what I believe);
Teaching me to love
And accept
All men and all things,
Through the life and death of Jesus Christ.

Can we risk it?

And so we build buildings
Of towers and spires,
Tall walls and stained glass windows;
With heavy doors and pews,
Beautiful buildings
Dedicated to God's work.

But God's work is people –
And that's more difficult
And costly to do,
Than raising money for buildings
And building them too;
Stones don't answer back
Or have opinions of their own.

And when the forms
Of a generation pass,
The buildings remain –
Preserving things as they were.

Living things grow and change
And flower and bear fruit,
So what of our church buildings?

Outreach

Most of our outreach
Is inreach,
Internal games, that reach only ourselves
Or those already inside.

We may even open our doors
To let others in
(One way traffic only)
Then try to persuade them
To come in,
But we seldom venture out.

It's not safe out there,
It's lonely –
There are many doubts out there,
One can't be so positive.

But there are people, out there,
And where people are,
God is.

Loveless

I believe God is against sin
(I will call it sin for want of a better word)
Not only because of the grief and pain
It causes him,
But because of the grief and pain
It causes us.

God loves us.
When we are hurt
He is hurt,
What hurts us, hurts him –
Like parent and child.

(Sin can be described as
An action without love.)

Canvass

Another canvass – stewardship campaign,
Based on love,
But is it?

The old lady who shuts her door quickly,
The lady who won't open the door
But speaks out the window,
The people who won't answer
The canvasser's knock, at all –
Show a strange response
To love.

Maybe they don't recognize
The stewardship campaign
For what it is?
Maybe they do?

Isn't there a gap
That can only be bridged
With understanding and concern –

For most people
Respond to – love,
And most people
Have no difficulty, in recognizing
Love.

To love and survive

Why do we flee into our churches
Away from the world?
Closing the doors
And shutting the world out –

Why don't we open the doors
And let the world into our churches?
The good and bad, the known and unknown,
The half understood,
Just as it is –
And ask God to help us cope,
And give us strength
To love – and survive.

To be a Christian

Why is it
That the last thing most of us Christians
Will dare to be – is a Christian?

We'll go to meetings,
We'll go to church, sing in the choir,
Have fellowship together,
Provide sandwiches,
Run crèches while meetings are on,
Have coffee mornings,
Attend seminars, lectures, rallies –
You name it.

But to love God
And our neighbour as ourselves?
To feed the hungry
And help the oppressed in my own town?
To lay myself open,
Enter someone else's sufferings –
And suffer with them?

Unnecessary martyrs

The church service tonight
Made me think
Of a glorious ship
Way out in the ocean –
Sinking.

Sinking slowly
In a stately manner
With all the crew and the passengers
On deck, standing to attention
Singing.

Ignoring
The rafts, the life-boats,
Which are there, ready
To save.

And take us to land

Where we could renew ourselves,
And build –
Another ship.

Some church establishments

Nobody knows but us,
Nobody knows but us,
Of morals and laws
And human flaws,
Of commands divine
And unshakeable.

We have shut our eyes
Our ears and our hearts
To the anguished cry of the lost,
We have set up standards
Most men can't reach,
Then said, 'Do this
Or be destroyed.'

We've not shared with people –

We've not bothered to seek
New standards for the new world,
That love (the only law) demands,
We've avoided the struggle –
The trial and suffering,
And hidden behind
Our duty.

Ruins

Ruins,
Far greater than many of the buildings
We cherish today,
More costly in sweat and toil,
With no modern materials
Or huge machines to help.

Must have taken decades to build –
Men must have hustled and worried
To keep the buildings going, keep them in order;
Power must have dwelt in them,
They are so big.
And now this –
Only an old stone ruin
Gaunt against the sky,
Whistling in the wind.

Do we fray our nerves,
Crease our brows,
Make our cheeks tight and pale
For this?

It seems neither the stones nor the buildings
Nor the power
Nor the organization
Were eternal –

Only the acts of love.

The empty horseshoe

What does the empty space
In front of the minister in church
Mean?

The gap between minister and layman?
Keeping a respectable distance from authority?
Since you can't argue with him
It's best not to get too close?

It doesn't happen between
A father and his family –
A shepherd and his flock.

God's world

I find more of God
In many secular songs,
Than I do in many hymns.

Somehow they're more real –
Maybe it's because
They don't have to be respectable,
Suitable, approved by the board.
They're down to earth
(Like Jesus)
With genuine joy and sorrow,
Made for ordinary people.
(God loves us all, remember.)

Somehow they communicate,
And I feel at one with
The people in the world,
Part of them,
Part of God's world.

Cup of tea

That cup of tea after the early service
Was good.

We weren't
  being pious,
  trying to solve financial problems,
  pressure-izing,
  worrying,
  projecting an image.

We were
  easy,
  ourselves,
  sharing,
  just being together.

The right things the wrong way

They say that we hide
From the problems of this world
In drugs and sport,
In culture and religion –
Not many have looked at it
This way.

But the man could be right,
We could be using,
The right things
The wrong way.

We could hide in our team,
In our art, in our creed,
Filling all our free moments with these;
Never once venturing outside
Our known circles.

But God is reliable –
And the things we've mentioned
Are there to strengthen us
For going out.
They're not
For hiding in.

We almost made it

We almost made it.
The local church almost decided to do something dangerous,
To break its bonds
And mix with the people in the world.

One couldn't tell which way
All the meetings and seminars were going to go,
Whether it would be the same old thing
Or whether we'd break out
And live dangerously,
Break out – and live.

But no, in the end
It was all watered down,
A small move here, a small move there –
Still bound by the same chains.

More

Once there was a man
Who made a better mousetrap,
And the world beat a path to his door.

Once there was a man
Who showed more love,
And the world has followed him since.

Once there was a church,
And it was empty.

Wedded

How many of us
Are studying, searching
To understand
This day and age,
Taking time to think
On Christianity, life and its problems?

How many of us have grasped
The basics
Of Faith, Hope, Love (and Forgiveness),
Or has it seemed too dangerous
And we've been content
Just to be good people?

There are two things:
The reality of Christ,
The reality of today,
And when they are wedded
We find Christianity.

The man

In the church we tried to hold him –
But there he wouldn't stay,
He broke free from our bindings
Cutting loose in his own way.

We tried to make him fit the mould
Of our denominations,
We tried to tie him up
In our creeds and regulations,
But somehow, he slipped away ...

We tried to pin him down
To the ways in which we saw him –
To our culture, laws and time –

We built huge buildings
And put him inside,
But he refused to hide.

We made him respectable,
Pious and learned, and may he
Well have been –
Even here, he has reached out
Beyond our safe limits.

We built institutions
Of love and care,
And tried to shackle him
Even there –

We explained him in books
With notes and pages,
And here too
He knows no gauges.

He's in the world –
He hasn't waited for us.

In aboriginal poetry,
In pop-music's stomping,
In the back streets and the palaces,
In discussions among unchurched men.
He walks the city streets,
Speaks on television
Along with going to church.

United by time
And culture and places,
He moves with love –
Christ.

A spade's a spade

Why is it that
Nearly every church meeting is reported as
Successful,
That it was enjoyed by all,
Warm fellowship was experienced,
An excellent talk was given,
Good progress was made,
The committee dealt keenly
With the problems to be tackled,
The situation offered an exciting challenge?

Don't we believe in freedom of speech?
Can there be no faults in our gatherings
Because all who attend are Christians?
Are we afraid to name our own weaknesses?

How can we grow if we can't face
Failure as well as success,
If we can't face what's bad
As well as what's good in our meetings?

The 'Good News' is that God loves us
Now,
Exactly as we are
Now,
With all our strengths and weaknesses.

Maybe we can learn to do the same
For ourselves and our fellow men;
Calling a spade a spade,
For growth must have its roots in reality –
That is, in God.

Thoughts

The only one can put you in contact with God,
Is someone who is already in contact with him.

I wonder if feelings that are pure, just, loving,
Are prayers that communicate.

People are refusing to be inspired,
For the sake of being inspired.

Too many of us
Are members of the institution first
And Christians second.

Let us pray for those who try

We so often only pray
For people in trouble.

Let us pray also
For the loving,
The joyful,
The kind and
The courageous.

The church

The church is like a garden –
A cultivated thing –
An agreement between servant and master
On how to raise the flowers
And make the vegetables grow.

It's communion between
People and God,
It's communion between
People and people.
Any people, all people, one people,
Good people, bad people,
In other words just plain people.

The church is really reality
Working through love and law,
Dying to live
Like the seed it sows,
Never knowing
Whither it goes –
Just trusting.

3 About life

Life

Life is now
This moment,
What I can see, hear, feel,
Now
Here.

In me and around me
With what I have,
With things just as they are –
Now.

Thoughts by the sea

Life is wonderful
And far more dangerous
Than the office –
(The breakers curl in
Glistening, murmuring, singing
Over the flat sand).

And so we have given up
The fun and excitement,
The beauty and joy – of living –
For safety;
Or what we regard as safety.

What in our world is secure:
Our home, our business, our community?
Surely the only security
Lies within us?
(The kids are coloured dots
On a huge sand dune,
Sliding down.)

The sea is living, dangerous, mysterious –
Yet,
The seagulls seem to manage.

Failure

What is wrong with failure?
A glorious failure –
I mean, to fail well
Means you've got to put in tremendous effort in the first
place,
And having gone to all this effort and trouble
Look at what you have learned,
What experience you have gained,
What knowledge from trial and error you have,
How very much farther on you are,
Than if you had never ventured –
And risked failure.
And now that calamity and collapse have blessed your ven-
ture,
You're still in one piece,
Been through the storm,
More knowledgeable, more calm, more humble,
More mature and likely to succeed the next time –
And maybe you will have learned something about faith.

The price is too high

The price is too high, for
The position that's offered,
And the power and security that
Go with it.
The price is too high, for
The salary offered,
It's too high a price, to pay
For money.

The price is the time, I have
With my wife and children
With some energy left to spend.
The price is the time, I have
To stop –
And find myself.

For what money or power, is worth
My freedom,
The values I hold,
My self respect?

It must be somebody else

Who me?
No, I'm not responsible
It must be somebody else –
They ought to be doing something about it.
They ought, you know,
I can't do anything.
Me, I'm no one.
It's them that's responsible
They're the leaders.
What us?
What, get together and register a protest?
Us? Not like them students,
But, but –
But I'd have to give up a night at the club
And there's a fight on tele tonight.
Me? Study the problem
Examine all sides of the question
Expose myself to questions and doubt
Make a decision
And be responsible?
No, not me –
It's them, I tell you,
It's them that's responsible.

Alone

It is difficult to express love
When alone.

Of no value?

Everything is measured in money –
In pounds and pence
In dollars and cents,
And if it can't be measured thus,
It's of no value.

Love has no value.
Beauty has no value.
Peace has no value.

For they are invaluable.

To respond

To visibly or invisibly acknowledge
Someone or their action,
To transmit to them
That you know –

Then they, knowing
That you know,
Respond
And it grows.

The petition

A pen (on a table)
Lying beside a piece of paper
On which there is a statement – a request –
Followed by some signatures.

No hiding,
Each name naked on the paper
For all to see.

A voice,
An act,
A daring to question authority –

The pen is mightier than the sword.

Roughage

Just as the bowel needs roughage to move it,
So does the mind.
It's inclined to get sluggish
On a diet of
Too much refined food.

Unpolished

So often, the unpolished
 the disjointed
Is on its way to the truth,
Ahead of the finished
 the polished.

Which half?

I must concentrate
On the half of my argument
That is right,
And the half of his argument
That is wrong,
And so we can argue
For ever –

But if I could add
The half of his argument
That is right,
To the half of my argument
That is right,
We could move
Towards
A solution.

Scales

When you push one side
Of a scales
Out of balance,
You can see the other
Side of the question
Go further in the other direction.

Deeds and words

Why is it that what men do
(Or are planning to do),
Always stands in front
Of what they say?

I wish I didn't know.

I wish I could believe
All the words,
They want me to believe;
All the words,
They want to believe
Themselves.

Pure metal

Pure metal
Does not only depend entirely
On how pure
The original ore was,
But also on how good
The refining process.

Beyond this line you shall not go

Once a line is drawn
There's a beginning and an end,
There's our side
And their side.

There's right and wrong,
(And we're usually right)
Black and white,
Two sides.

Nature has few straight lines.

If no line is drawn
There are no sides –
No limits.

Maybe the answer lies in
Temporary, flexible lines,
When we can find no alternative
For the present, to
Drawing lines.

Keeping the door open

How I'd like to close that door –
But if I did,
They'd have to knock
And ask to come in;
Then they wouldn't come so freely.

That's what counts

How difficult it is to trust our own judgment
How difficult it is to think we are right,
After all we are no one important –
Inexperienced.

And yet we have a certain feeling
Hard to define and trace it out,
Hard to express in good clear sentences,
And so we give in –
Or keep quiet,
Thinking others must know more than us;
Not trusting ourselves
When we can't express
The thing that we feel – clearly.

But trust ourselves we should
Our thoughts and fears and doubts,
Just as they are
They're ours, they're us,
And that's what counts –
Not what the others think.

By wavering – we're easy meat,
But positive positive or positive doubt
Or half way in between,
It's our opinion, and
That's what counts.

Eternal

No matter what field your work lies in
If you do something real
Something genuine in that field,
It will live on after you –
And that part of you will be eternal.

The meaning

Once, man found a meaning
And clothed it, as best he could,
In words.

With new knowledge
From more seeking
The meaning grew,
For some;
The rest found the old words
So comfortable,
They kept the old words
And stifled the new meaning.

A definition of vandalism for today

Any action
That destroys some useful or beautiful thing,
Without making money out of it.

Tear it down

Tear it down, tear it down,
It has no place in this town,
It's standing in the way
Of progress.

The trees are pleasant
Standing there,
But just think of the new hotel –
And all the people it will bring –
And all the money.

That was a slum area
We're cleaning out,
And putting a new road through;
We're shifting the people
Further out – further out – further out.
(They may find it hard to make new friends,
And they'll need a car to get to work –
Making the problems even worse.)

And now the old buildings must make way,
For our newer, brighter offices –
They may have been historic and beautiful too,
But after all they're not very new!
And who'd pay for their upkeep?
You can't stop progress.

So now some streets
Are narrow brick canyons,
Crammed, and noisy, and hurried;
Untouched by the sun, and filled with smoke,

With no light, nor beauty, nor life –
Unfit for human habitation.
What made our people anti-social?

Not knowing

I envied her
Her youth and fun,
The freedom that she took
So lightly.

Until I met her
On her day off –
Walking the streets alone.

Poverty

Two migrant women –
(Mother and daughter)
Their faces marked
By dark shadows
Under their eyes.

Waiting,
(With the children)
In an old car
Outside,
A real estate office.

Too ordinary

'Are you going away for the holidays?'

'Yes, I've hired a house by the beach,
What about you?'

'I'll be going to
My ordinary house
In my ordinary street
Because of my ordinary wages.'

Hawthorn tree

Last night I saw a hawthorn tree.
I knew it would bud soon –
And yet there was no sign
Nothing to show –
Just an ordinary bare branch.

Then I wondered
How many people I knew
Were like that twig?
Seemingly bare and barren,
Showing no promise,
Who would suddenly
Burst into life
And beauty and strength –
With me having
No hand in it whatsoever.

Pop-music

Pop-music – the voice of the people.

Harsh, discordant, chaotic –
Maybe,
For that is the world they're forced to live in,
So, these things must be expected –
But
Always
(No matter what the country, the religion,
... the regime,)
You'll find
Beauty, truth, love,
Joy (and sadness) –
Life.

Listen,
Share –
And live with them,
For they tell
Of the world
As it is –
And as they hope
It may one day
BE.

Travellers

There must have been men
Who dreamed
Of climbing far off mountains,
Which they never reached –
Only travelled towards –
And no one knew.

There must be men like this today
I wish I knew.

Next spring

'Come next spring,' said David,
'We'll climb those hills together –'
He was my friend, and
Those were his last words to me.
Next spring came, but not David;
He was killed in a car accident.

Too often, we wait for spring.

Nothing

Once they had nothing
And they had everything,
Now they have everything
And they have nothing.

It's only Joe

'Oh, it's only Joe.'
Wiped with one sweep of the cloth.
Only?
Can anyone be only?
The translation of this sentence reads,
'It's only me.'
And even that's not correct.

Labels

We've got labels for this
And labels for that,
Each person and thing
Must fit
Into the space, provided.

He's a this, he's a that,
He's the other,
Not safe till he's packaged and labelled.
And we don't feel at ease
Till we know what he is –
The sooner he's branded the better.

And if he should step
Out of his box
And utter a statement
Or act in a manner,
That won't fit with the image provided;
He's unreliable.

Deep down

We skate on ice
And we zip and zoom
Gliding and spinning and dancing,
We skate with others and socialize
And teach and learn and organize
(Community games) –
But it all takes place
On the surface.

We seldom go deep
Where the water's cold,
Deep, deep down
To the bottom.

Some never find out, what it's all about,
The whys and whens and wherefores;
For it's only on down
The answers lie,
Far beneath the surface.

That most difficult thing

That most difficult thing –
To see something
From someone else's point of view.

To let go of ourselves enough
To be able to care,
To let go enough
To be aware,
To let go enough
To sit still and listen
Intently –
Taking it all in . . .

The problem,
The person,
(His background)
The others involved –
Our own prejudices.

To get inside someone else's skin
And feel what they feel,
Their joy, their sorrow,
As though it were our own –
To know.

The roots

I must teach my children, the root
Of things.

Like,
People in poverty need more than charity;
To be released
They need jobs
And housing, health and education.

Gaoling
Drug addicts and sex offenders
Temporarily removes them from society,
It doesn't solve the problem.
Only study,
Understanding and correct treatment
Can do any lasting good.

The means should never be allowed
To become the end.

Certain

A certain type of person
Is only likely to communicate
With certain types of people,
Who only believe certain
Types of ideas.
And everyone they know
Believes
What they believe –
That everyone else
Is wrong.

Untapped

Each human being
Is a mine
Of knowledge and experience –
Untapped.

We do have a choice

Where are we going
When we rush about?
Pushing and worrying our way through,
To where?
With our stomachs in
And our faces grim.

Too many things to do,
Too many people to know,
Too many possessions to care for,
Too many luxuries to try and enjoy,
Too many decisions to make –
Not enough time.

No stopping place,
Or healing quiet,
No chance to get right out of the race
For a while.

But someone once said,
'When the bell rings
You don't have to answer.'
Did you ever think of that?
We don't have to go
When we're called –
We do have a choice.

A passing shadow

Like butterflies trapped
In a window pane,
Gently fluttering against
The cold glass,
Seeking an outlet that
Can't be found –
Quietly frantic.

Humans trapped in rigid systems
Seeking, hoping, trying –
Unable as yet to grasp
The unbreakable strength of the glass,
Against which
Their butterfly wings flutter.

Till maybe some power greater
Opens the window,
An accident shatters the glass,
Or the butterfly dies.

Listening

Have you listened to the silence
And wondered?
The water running in the next room, the distant car,
The chair creaking, your own breathing;
And been still.

Have you heard what someone is saying,
Beyond the words?
Felt the pain, the uncertainty, the misery,
The groping and searching
Even as your own.

Have you heard the birds singing at dawn?
Each one quietly joining the next
Until they are all awake,
And then to work.

Have you heard the noise in a factory,.
In a street, in a broken home?
Tearing at the nerves
Pressing in like a wall –
Till something breaks.

If you have heard
Men will be glad,
For to have heard
Is to be aware.

Communion

My soul was drifting
In a void,
Driving on an empty road –
When I heard a cry
'Oih!'
Then I saw them –
In a scattered bunch
Working by the edge of the road –
My old mates.

My soul warmed
And was cheered,
A smile broke out
On my face;
I waved
And had communion.

Filling up

Filling up with peace
Listening to the transistor,
Insects flutter on the window pane
And the 'fridge ticks over.

The cups on the table and the marmalade
Are quiet.
Everything blends, easily –
And slowly the peace fills up
Till my cup is full.

I couldn't find it
And yet it's always been here.
Often I've travelled far
Seeking, looking –
And now I find it, peace
Here.

Monotony

First cousin of loneliness,
The arch enemy,
Destroyer of will-power
Blunting the edge of effort,
Killing all hope.

Nothing to do –
Nothing new, no one new,
No new place, no new idea,
Same place, same time,
Same me, same you,
Nothing, nothing, nothing.

What are my answers?
Despite my surroundings
And companions
It lies with me –
To do something new,
Something I wouldn't normally do.
To take a risk,
Expose my real self,
And accept the hurt
With the rewards.

Problems

How can I solve my problems
If I do not know who I am
Or what I am?
If I can't answer the questions
'Who am I?'
'What am I?'
('Where have I come from?')

Someone said
Every man must solve the puzzle
Of his own life, for himself.

Or must I first lose myself
To find myself?

Surely the answer must lie in
Self knowledge –
To grow as best I can, in
My native soil.

Competition

Why must I prove that I'm better
Than you?
Why must you prove that you're better
Than me?
Why have I to be stronger
                braver
                cleverer
                faster, than you?
Why should I have to use you
To prove myself
To myself? (and to others?)

I can only measure my growth
Against how tall I was before.

And mostly
Only I know how tall I was before.

After the dark

It's dark now –
And I'm flying low,
Cold.
But deep within me
I remember
A darkness like this
That came before.

And I remember
That after that hard dark
That long dark –
Dawn broke.
And the sun rose
Again.

And that is what I must
Remember now.

Waiting

So much of it, consists of waiting,
Just waiting.

Waiting for maturity,
Waiting for recognition,
Waiting for health,
Waiting for opportunity –
For a beginning
Or an end.

Since so much of it
Does consist of waiting,
Maybe we should learn
How to wait,

How to live, while waiting.
The whole of life for some
May be one long wait,
So things must be done
And life has to be lived,
And peace and joy and fulfilment
Found –
While waiting.

And I will know it's right

Why must I do it?
Because it will be right.
But no one will take any notice
They don't care –
Because it will be right.
But they'll do what they want to do
It's up to them anyway –
Because it will be right.
I mean you can't go on
Being responsible for every thing,
The others won't worry –
Because it will be right.
No one else would do it
So why do I have to?
Because it will be right.

And I will know it's right.

Hello trouble

Hello trouble, (you – –)
I've met with you before –
So now you're here again,
Bigger than ever, larger than life,
Ready to cause more and more strife
And break me if you can.
My hands are tied behind my back
My legs they are in chains,
My health is not what it used to be
I do have aches and pains,
My responsibilities loom large
And there are those who on me depend
Whom I wouldn't see hurt for the world –
So buzz off trouble. But if you're going to stay:
My brow you may crease, my shoulders you may bow,
My mind you may scar, my nerves you may break,
Mark you I said MAY;
But mark also if you stay
I shall surely grow and grow,
And my spirit, my soul, you cannot touch,
For they belong to God and me –
And no matter what you do or say
They always will be free.

Love

Love, is glad when you are glad
Is sad when you are sad
Is hurt when you are.
Love is never so wrapped in himself
He can't listen to you,
And hear you.
Love accepts you exactly as you are –
Is happy for your strengths
Is sorry for you in your weakness,
(However unacceptable it may appear)
Stands beside you in your struggle.
Love knows no time
And is always available.
Love may criticize what you do
But never you,
And looks with you
For the right path, for you.
Love makes no judgments
And has a deep respect for you:
Love shares his all with you
His time, his possessions, his talents.
Love grows by sharing himself;
Love drives out fear;
Love is eternal and never dies;
Love cares.

To live

The story is not in the telling –
But in the living,
The pain is not in the recital –
But in the time;
Life cannot be bought, paid for, borrowed,
Only lived and accepted.

A beautiful figure is not
In a painting or sculpture,
But under a hand;
Some things you can't read about
And understand.

Hence the poorest is as rich as the rich –
In experience.
To love and be loved, needs no
Cars and palaces;
Only two people.

So many of our possessions
Belong to our self-protection racket,
Protecting us from experiencing reality –
Which would make us unafraid
And free to love, truly.

Freedom

Freedom
– from being driven,
– from fear,
– from seeking acceptance,
– from weariness,
– from a feeling that the task is impossible,
– from a feeling that communication is impossible,
– from wanting to change everything, immediately,
– from always wanting –
– from always wanting – freedom.

Free to love

To have no pride
And no humility,
To have no right
And no wrong,
To have no set path –
Only a guiding light.

To have no friends
And no enemies –
Only people to be loved.

So strange, so new

It's strange how
After all these last battles
I walk the earth as a stranger now.

The stars are bright, ever new,
The dust on the ground crunches friendly,
The trees and I are part of the whole –
And it's all so strange, so new.

Then

And someday I won't be tired
Not ever, any more,
Someday I'll be calm and free
And walk by the seashore;
It'll all be over
The thing will be done –
The fight will be won or lost.

Then shall I see more clearly
Then shall I really know,
How you have always loved me;
How you have always been here
Standing by my side.

I'll see how I needn't have worried
And tossed and turned about so,
I'll see that it all had a purpose
A way that it had to go;
I'll see that there was direction
Though at times I didn't think so –
And I'll be quiet.